The EASTER Book

Rita Storey

W
FRANKLIN WATTS
LONDON•SYDNEY

This edition 2014

Franklin Watts
338 Euston Road
London NW1 3BH

Franklin Watts Australia
Level 17/207 Kent Street
Sydney, NSW 2000

Editor: Paul Rockett
Design: Ruth Walton
Picture Research: Diana Morris
Illustrator: Shelagh McNicholas, pp 8–11
Commissioned photography: Paul Bricknell Photography,
   pp14, 18, 22–5, 28–30,
   32–40,43

Dewey number: 394.2'667

ISBN: 978 1 4451 3077 4

Printed in China

Franklin Watts is a division of
Hachette Children's Books,
an Hachette UK company.

www.hachette.co.uk

Picture credits:
AG foto/Shutterstock: 13bl; age fotostock/Superstock: 17cl; Alamy Celebrity/Alamy: 17tr; Vladimir Alexeer/Alamy: 37t; Argus//Shutterstock: 13tra, 21tlc, 21bla; Christopher Bernard/istockphoto: 25bl; blue orange studio /Shutterstock: 26tl; brulove/Shutterstock: 15cr; Cammeramnnz/Shutterstock: 15crb; George P Chroma/Shutterstock: 27tl; Leila Cutler/Alamy: 7clb; Daboost/Shutterstock: 12cra, 13cla; Martin Dallaire/Shutterstock: 42bl; Fenton/Shutterstock: 21clb; Douglas Freer/Shutterstock: 13tl; granata1111/Shutterstock: 20clb. Richard Griffin/Shutterstock. 21br; Irish Design/Shutterstock: 18bg, 22-23bg, 26-27bg, 30-31bg, 34-35bg, 44-45bg; Mark A Johnson/Alamy: 41br; Jorisvo/Shutterstock: 6tr; Jrtmedia/Dreamstime: 31b; Jack K/Shutterstock: 13tr; Wendy Kaveney Photography/Shutterstock: 12cl; Michael Kemp/Alamy: 15br; Jutta Klee/Corbis: 41tl; Pavle Marjanovic/Shutterstock: 13bla; Markova/Shutterstock: 6tl, 7b, 8t, 12t, 14t, 15bl, 19tl, 20t, 24t, 28t, 32t, 34t, 36t, 38t, 40t; Stewart Mckenzie/Shutterstock: back cover tr, 27br; Mordechai Meiri/Shutterstock: 40tr; Melaics/Shutterstock: 14-15 bg, 36-37 bg, 46-47 bg; Aleksandar Mijatovic/Shutterstock: 12bl, 21tr; Mode Images/Alamy: 6b; Edward Marques-Mortimer/Dreamstime: 12cr; nito/Shutterstock: 20cl; 1000 words/Shutterstock: 6cl; Alexander Ozerov/Shutterstock: 7t; andere andrea petrik/Shutterstock: 3tl, 4bl, 4br, 6clb, 7bl, 7bra, 7br,19trb, 21tla, 25blb, 28brb, 32tl, 33bl, 44tr; Dan Ionut Popsecu/Shutterstock: 32-33 bg, 38-39 bg; A & N Protasov/Shutterstock: 16br; Dianka Pyzhova/Shutterstock: front cover c; Lev Radin/Shutterstock: 42cl, 42cr, 42br; Stephen Aaron Rees/Shutterstock: 12cla; Rex Features: 26b; ruskpp/Shutterstock: 13crb; Shining Colors/Dreamstime: 7cl; Ariel Skelley/Alamy: 7c; Slick Shoots/Alamy: 13cl; Snake 8/Dreamstime: 16tr; Southmind/Shutterstock: 12br; Ant Strack/Corbis: 41cl; Studio Barcelona/Shutterstock: 21bl; Allan Suddaby . www.buttonsoup.ca <http://www.buttonsoup.ca> : 13cr; Homer Sykes/Alamy: 16tl; Luboslav Tiles/Shutterstock: 12bla; Nico Tondini/Robert Harding: 21trb; toriru /Shutterstock: 38bl; Hugh Trelfal/Alamy: 17trb; Gerge Tsartsianidis/Dreamstime: 21cl; Peter 21jlstra/Shutterstock: 21tlb; VectorARA/Shutterstock: 19b; Christian Vinces/Shutterstock: 19tr; Edward Westmacott/Shutterstock: 17br; Daniel Wiedeman/Shutterstock: 15cl; Gary Woods/Alamy: 15tl; Yui/Shutterstock: 12bra, 13tla, 21cra; Zolssa/Shutterstock: 4-5 bg, 24-25 bg, 28-29 bg, 40-41bg, 43bg; Zuma Press/Alamy: 16cl, 31t; Zush/Shutterstock: 36tl.

Contents

What is Easter?

Easter is celebrated by millions of people all over the world. But why? Where does it come from?

A celebration of Jesus

Easter Sunday celebrates the most important event in the Christian calendar, the resurrection (rising from the dead) of Jesus after he was crucified (put to death on a cross). The Friday before Easter Sunday is Good Friday. This is the day that Christians believe Jesus was crucified. Two days later, on Easter Sunday, they believe that Jesus came back from the dead.

A celebration of spring

It is thought that the word Easter may come from *Eostre*, the name of a goddess of spring from northern Europe. Long before the birth of Jesus, people celebrated the arrival of spring. In spring the trees blossom and begin to grow new leaves, baby animals are born, and crops begin to grow. People relied on the return of spring for the crops and they worshipped many gods and goddesses associated with this season.

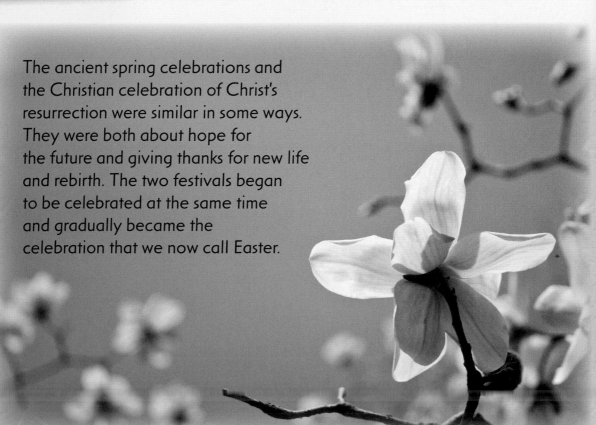

The ancient spring celebrations and the Christian celebration of Christ's resurrection were similar in some ways. They were both about hope for the future and giving thanks for new life and rebirth. The two festivals began to be celebrated at the same time and gradually became the celebration that we now call Easter.

6

When is Easter?

The date of Easter changes every year. It is worked out from when the first full moon happens after 21 March. The Sunday after the full moon is Easter Sunday. This means the date of Easter Sunday can be anywhere from 22 March to 25 April.

How do you celebrate Easter?

People celebrate Easter in different ways around the world. Which part of Easter do you enjoy most?

Symbols of spring

Spring is a time when plants and animals come to life again after the cold days of winter. Lambs and Easter bunnies are symbols of spring. This is because these animals have their babies in spring when there is fresh grass to feed them. Hens lay more eggs in spring and some of them will hatch into fluffy yellow spring chicks. Spring flowers are the first flowers to bloom after winter. Their bright colours remind us of spring sunshine and blue skies.

The Easter story

The Easter story tells us about the resurrection of Jesus.

Jesus had been preaching God's word and healing the sick in towns and villages all over Palestine. His followers loved him, but he also had many enemies, especially in the city of Jerusalem.

God wanted Jesus to go to Jerusalem, and Jesus knew that going there would mean certain death. On the way he warned his disciples that he would soon die.

Just before they came to the city, Jesus sent for a donkey. There was a prophecy that God would send a Messiah (a King of the Jews) who would save mankind and that he would enter Jerusalem riding on a donkey.

As Jesus rode into Jerusalem, fulfilling God's prophecy, the crowds went wild. They shouted in celebration and threw palm leaves down in front of him.

Some of the priests were very unhappy that Jesus was so popular and wanted him dead. They offered Judas, one of Jesus' disciples, thirty pieces of silver to betray his friend. Judas took the money.

Later that week Jesus and his twelve disciples sat down to a Passover meal together. Jesus explained that the next day he would be arrested and killed, but that the disciples should not be sad because he would be going to heaven. Jesus also said that one of them had already betrayed him. The disciples did not believe him, but Judas and Jesus both knew the truth.

Jesus broke some bread and shared it around saying, 'Take and eat; this is my body.' Then he offered them a cup of wine and told them that it symbolised his blood.

That night Jesus went with some of his disciples to the Garden of Gethsemane to pray. In the morning, Judas arrived with guards and soldiers. The guards arrested Jesus and took him to Pontius Pilate, the Roman leader.

Pontius Pilate did not want to put Jesus to death. He offered the crowd a choice of freeing a man named Barabbas or Jesus.

Barabbas was a murderer, while Jesus' only crime was to say that he was the Son of God. But the priests persuaded the crowd to demand that Jesus be crucified. Pilate released Barabbas but washed his hands in front of the crowd to show that he was innocent of Jesus' death.

Jesus was given a crown of sharp thorns to wear on his head. He was made to drag a large wooden cross to the top of a nearby hill. The soldiers nailed Jesus to the cross and raised it up with a sign saying, 'The King of the Jews'.

That night Jesus died. As he did so the earth shook with a great earthquake.

Jesus' friends took his body and laid it in a tomb cut from the side of a hill. They rolled a heavy stone across the entrance to seal it.

Two days later a friend of Jesus called Mary Magdalen went to visit the tomb. When she got there she was amazed to find the stone rolled away from the entrance. Inside there was no sign of Jesus' body.

Mary told the disciples what had happened and they went to see for themselves. Mary stayed alone crying. Two angels then appeared before her and asked why she was crying.
As she told them, she turned and saw
Jesus standing before her.

Jesus appeared to all the disciples saying, 'Go into the world, and preach the gospel to everyone.' Then he went up to heaven to be with God.

Shrove Tuesday

Shrove Tuesday is the day before Lent. Lent is a period during which people prepare for Easter. Some people give up certain foods. Traditionally, Shrove Tuesday was the day when people held feasts to use up all the food they were not allowed to eat for Lent. These foods included red meat, eggs, sugar and butter. Some parts of the world have spectacular celebrations on Shrove Tuesday.

Mardi Gras

In New Orleans and Louisiana in the United States, Shrove Tuesday is called Mardi Gras (Fat Tuesday). Millions of people go every year to watch the decorated floats that parade through the streets, and to dance and party.

In Rio de Janeiro, Brazil, the Mardi Gras celebration is called Carnival and people party and dance to samba music.

In Venice, Italy, people dress in beautiful costumes and disguises to attend masked balls.

In Nice, France, the Mardi Gras lasts for ten days. People wear crazy masks and there are parades and street theatre performances.

Pancake Day

In Great Britain and Ireland another name for Shrove Tuesday is Pancake Day. Eggs and milk are combined with flour to make a batter. The batter is cooked in butter in a flat pan and called a pancake.

In other parts of the world there are recipes designed to use up rich ingredients before Lent. In Poland they make *paczki*, a type of doughnut fried in oil.

In Australia they eat a type of pancake that is thicker than the ones in Great Britain. They are served cold, with butter or jam and cream.

Parts of Canada make pancakes and bake small objects into them. The items are symbolic of what will happen over the next year – coins symbolize wealth, a ring a wedding. The pancakes are served with sausages and partridgeberry jam. This is a type of jam made from small red berries that grow wild in Canada and the United States.

In Sweden they eat a type of round bun which has the middle scooped out to be filled with marzipan and thick cream.

Pancakes

Pancakes are great fun to make and delicious to eat. See how high you can toss a pancake, and if it doesn't stick to the ceiling, you can enjoy eating it with savoury or sweet fillings.

Make a perfect pancake

Ingredients:

* 110g plain flour
* a pinch of salt
* 1 egg
* 275ml milk
* butter for frying

You will need:

* a sieve
* a cup
* a large bowl
* a hand whisk
* a tablespoon
* a jug
* a frying pan
* a fish slice
* a plate

Instructions:

1. Sift the flour and salt into a bowl.
2. Crack the egg into a cup. Make a hole in the centre of the mixture and pour in the egg.
3. Add a little of the milk and mix well with a hand whisk.
4. Add the rest of the milk gradually, mixing all the time. Pour the mixture into a jug.

Hot fat is very dangerous so you will need a grown-up to help with this.

5. Add a little piece of butter to a hot frying pan.
6. Pour in 2–3 tablespoons of the mixture.
7. Swirl the pan round gently so that the base of the pan is coated with the mixture. Leave for 2–3 minutes until it is almost set.
8. Flip the pancake over with a fish slice. Cook for a further 2–3 minutes.
9. Slide the pancake out onto a plate.

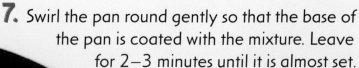

To toss a pancake

The trick is not to toss the pancake too high until you get the technique right.

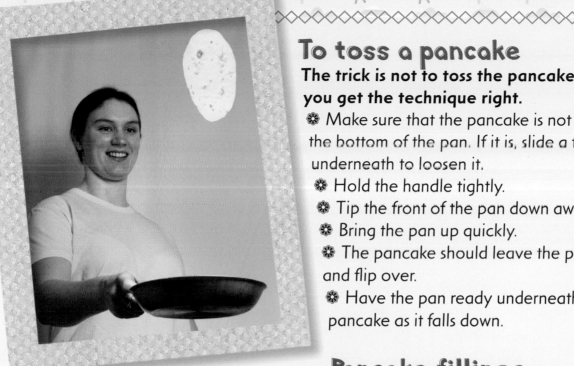

❋ Make sure that the pancake is not stuck to the bottom of the pan. If it is, slide a fish slice underneath to loosen it.

❋ Hold the handle tightly.

❋ Tip the front of the pan down away from you.

❋ Bring the pan up quickly.

❋ The pancake should leave the pan, turn and flip over.

❋ Have the pan ready underneath the pancake as it falls down.

Pancake fillings

Pancakes in Great Britain are traditionally served with a squeeze of lemon juice and a sprinkle of sugar. There are lots of other ways to enjoy pancakes. Try these yummy fillings:

❋ **raspberries and ice cream with a drizzle of raspberry sauce**

❋ **sliced banana and ice cream**

❋ **banana and maple syrup.**

Pancake races

Some places hold pancake races on Shrove Tuesday. In a pancake race the runners must toss the pancake a given number of times whilst running to the finish line. This tradition is supposed to have started when a woman heard the church bell ringing on Shrove Tuesday and ran to church with her pancake still cooking in the pan.

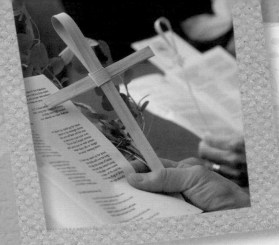

All about Lent

The 40 days (not including Sundays) leading up to Easter are called Lent. There are many days celebrated during this time. Find out about them on the next few pages.

The 40 days of Lent

Jesus spent 40 days in the desert to prepare for God's work. During that time he did not eat and was tempted by the Devil. Jesus was very strong and did not give in to temptation. In remembrance of that time Christians try to eat very little and some eat no meat at all during the 40 days before Easter. Many people give up treats, such as chocolate or cakes, during this time.

Ash Wednesday

This is the first day of Lent. Ash is what is left behind when something has been burned. It is a symbol of being sorry. On Ash Wednesday the priest blesses the ash that is left from burning the remaining palm crosses from the previous year. The ash is used to make the sign of a cross on the forehead of people as a sign that they are sorry for things they have done wrong in the past year.

Palm Sunday

Palm Sunday is the beginning of the week before Easter. This last week is called Holy Week. On Palm Sunday we remember when Jesus entered Jerusalem riding on a donkey. On entering Jerusalem, people laid down palm leaves before him and because of this Christian churches hold a service where palm leaves are blessed. The palm leaves are then made into crosses.

Maundy Thursday

This is the last Thursday of Lent, the day before Good Friday when Jesus was crucified. On this day Christians remember Jesus' Last Supper. During the Last Supper, Jesus shared bread and wine with his disciples, and in church services people remember this act by also sharing bread and wine. Today, in Great Britain the Queen gives out coins called Maundy money on Maundy Thursday.

In the Spanish town of Verges they hold a skeleton dance called *La Dansa de la Mort*. For this, people dress up in skeleton costumes and dance to the beat of a drum to symbolise death.

Good Friday

On Good Friday, Christians all over the world remember Jesus being crucified on the cross. Many people go to church services and some people fast completely to remember what Jesus sacrificed for them. Churches are not decorated and statues and pictures are covered up. It is traditional to eat hot cross buns on Good Friday. They are spicy buns with a pastry cross on the top. This symbolises the cross upon which Jesus was crucified.

Make a palm cross

Make your own palm cross as a decoration for Palm Sunday.

You will need:
* a strip of green or yellow paper 42cm long x 1cm wide at the bottom, tapering to a point at the other end
* a ruler
* sticky tape

Instructions:

1. Lay the strip of paper on a flat surface with the pointed end at the top and fold the point down to make a fold 10cm from the bottom. Fold the pointed end up and out at a right angle 4cm from the top.

2. Fold the paper to the back, 2.5cm along the front horizontal strip.

3. Fold that paper towards you to make an arm the same length as the one on the right (2.5cm). This is the shape of the cross. Fold the pointed end up and away from you between the top and right branches of the cross.

4. Fold it down behind the cross.

5. Fold it across the front,

6. Fold it back and up between the top and left branches of the cross.

7. Tuck the point through the piece of paper under the horizontal branches. Trim the excess paper and secure with sticky tape.

Easter Sunday

This is a happy day as Christians remember Jesus rising from the dead. Many Christians go to church on Easter Sunday. The celebrations may begin with a Sunrise Service to watch the sun come up.

Non-Christians and Christians alike celebrate the idea of rebirth on Easter Sunday by eating Easter eggs. Traditionally these were birds' eggs, but modern Easter eggs are larger and usually of the chocolate variety!

Easter Sunday around the world

Easter Sunday is a holiday in many countries with people giving each other gifts of eggs. In Great Britain and the USA these are usually made of chocolate. In Germany, Ukraine and Poland they are likely to be beautifully decorated hens' eggs.

As well as exchanging eggs people also get together to have fun with other egg-related traditions. Hunting for eggs is a popular pastime on Easter Sunday. In towns and villages in Europe, Australia and the USA the Easter Bunny hides eggs for children to find (see page 41).

In Great Britain, the USA and Germany egg rolling is popular. The idea is to see who can roll a hard-boiled egg the greatest distance down a slope without it breaking (see page 26).

The period of time before Easter Sunday used to be a time of fasting and wearing plain clothing. On Easter Sunday people could wear bright colours and their best clothes again to celebrate the resurrection. The new hats that they wore became more and more decorated and villages began to have Easter bonnet parades. Spectacular Easter parades are held around the world today. The biggest is held in New York City (see page 42).

Easter food

Many Christians give up rich foods during Lent and either fast or eat fish instead of meat on Ash Wednesday and Good Friday. Many non-Christians try to give up chocolate or sweets for Lent and have adopted the ritual of eating fish rather than meat on Good Friday. It is not surprising that everyone is ready for a feast when Easter Sunday arrives. Lamb and eggs are eaten in many countries but some countries have their own special dishes.

United States of America

In the USA, ham is often eaten at Easter rather than lamb. This tradition came about because before fridges were invented, any pork not eaten during the winter was cured (preserved). The cured meat was ready to eat at about Easter time – just right for a celebratory meal.

Spain

A popular food eaten in Spain at Easter is the *torrijas*. This is made from slices of warm bread soaked in milk, sugar and egg, then fried in olive oil. The crisp slices are served with syrup, honey, sugar or cinnamon. In parts of Spain they also eat cakes called *Mona de Pascua* (left). These cakes used to be given to godchildren by their godparents. They were decorated with boiled eggs. Today's Mona de Pascua have gone crazy – many of them are more like elaborate chocolate sculptures!

France

Lamb is traditionally cooked for the main Easter meal in France, and served with spring vegetables. The French eat Easter fish as well as beautifully decorated eggs.

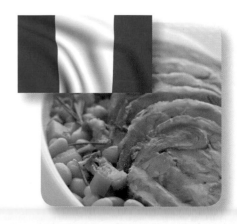

In many countries people bake special bread or buns at Easter. Bread is a symbol of Jesus as he broke bread with the disciples at the Last Supper.

Holland

The Dutch eat *Paasbrood*, a loaf with a paste of almonds in the centre.

Italy

In Italy loaves are decorated with coloured eggs.

Greece

Tsoureki is the traditional Easter bread in Greece. It is braided into a crown and decorated with hard-boiled eggs, dyed red.

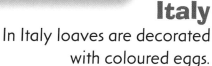

Great Britain

In Great Britain hot cross buns decorated with a cross are eaten on Good Friday.

Poland

In Poland people eat a spongy sweet bread called *babka*.

JOKE!
What do you get when you pour coffee down a rabbit hole?

Hot cross bunnies!

21

Make hot cross buns

Hot cross buns are delicious to eat hot or cold. These buns are a bit tricky to make so you will need a grown-up to help you.

Ingredients:

* 450g strong plain flour
* 3 teaspoons fast action dried yeast
* 1 teaspoon salt
* 1 level teaspoon mixed spice
* 25g currants
* 25g chopped mixed peel
* 75g caster sugar
* 200ml milk
* 50g melted butter
* 1 egg

To glaze the top of the buns:
* 40g sugar
* 2 tablespoons water

You will need:

* a large bowl
* a jug
* a wooden spoon
* cling film
* a pastry brush
* two baking trays
* a rolling pin
* a kitchen knife
* wire cooling rack
* a kettle

Instructions:

1. Put all the dried ingredients, including the yeast, into a bowl and make a hollow in the middle.

2. Mix the egg and milk in a jug and pour into the hollow. Pour in the melted butter and mix with a wooden spoon.

3. When it becomes one big lump of dough, mix it together with your hands. Add a bit more flour if it is sticky.

4. Put the dough on a floured work surface and ask a grown-up to help you knead the dough until it is smooth.

5. Put the mixture back into the bowl and cover the bowl with cling film. Leave the bowl somewhere warm for about an hour.

6. Preheat the oven to 200°C.

7. Brush two baking trays with a little bit of oil to stop the buns sticking to them.

8. Divide the dough into 12 pieces and shape them into buns. Put the buns on the baking tray, leaving a space between each one. Put them in a warm place until they have doubled in size.

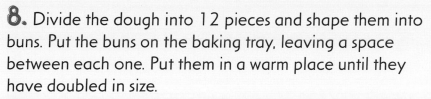

9. Mix 110g of plain flour with 3 tablespoons of water until it becomes a lump of dough.

10. Roll the mixture out thinly. Cut into thin strips with a kitchen knife.

11. Brush a bit of water onto the strips. Stick them onto the buns in the shape of a cross.

12. Put the trays of buns into the oven, on or above the middle shelf. Bake for 15-20 minutes. Take out of the oven (with oven gloves) and leave the buns to cool on a wire rack.

13. Measure 40g caster sugar into a bowl. Boil some water in a kettle and add two tablespoons of the boiling water to the sugar. Stir until the sugar has dissolved. Brush the mixture onto the buns while they are still warm.

Try toasting a bun and spreading it with butter... Yummy!

Simnel cake

Simnel cake is a light fruitcake covered in marzipan. On the top of the cake are eleven marzipan balls to represent the disciples of Jesus. Judas is not included because he was the disciple who betrayed Jesus. The recipe for Simnel cake is very old. There are records of these cakes being made since medieval times.

You will need:

❀ a large bowl
❀ a sieve
❀ a metal spoon
❀ a rolling pin
❀ a kitchen knife
❀ 18cm cake tin
❀ baking paper
❀ wire cooling rack
❀ a pastry brush
❀ a skewer

Ingredients:

❀ 175g butter or margarine
❀ 175g caster sugar
❀ 3 large eggs
❀ 225g plain flour
❀ 1 teaspoon ground cinnamon
❀ 425g mixed dried fruit
❀ 1-2 tablespoons milk
❀ 500g marzipan
❀ apricot jam

Instructions:

1. Preheat the oven to 170°C.

2. Mix the butter and sugar together and beat in the eggs a bit at a time.

3. Sieve the flour and cinnamon into the mixture. Fold it in gently with a metal spoon, then fold in the fruit.

4. Mix to a soft mixture with a little milk. Grease the cake tin with a little butter. Put half the mixture into the tin and level it off with a spoon.

5. Divide the marzipan into three pieces.

6. Roll out one of the three pieces on a board dusted with icing sugar to form a circle a bit smaller than the tin.

7. Place the marzipan circle on top of the cake mixture.

8. Cover the marzipan with the rest of the cake mixture and level it off with a kitchen knife. Ask a grown-up to tie a band of paper round the outside of the tin and 5cm above it to stop the top of the cake getting too brown.

9. Put the tin in the oven and bake for 1 hour. Place the skewer through the centre of the cake. If the skewer is clean then the cake is done, otherwise turn the heat down to 150°C and cook for a further 15–30 minutes.

10. Let the cake cool in the tin. Turn it out onto a wire rack.

11. Roll out one of the pieces of marzipan into a circle to put on the top of the cake.

12. Brush the apricot jam over the top of the cake and press on the marzipan circle.

13. Roll the last piece of marzipan into a sausage and cut it into 11 equal pieces. Roll the pieces into small balls.

14. Brush the top and sides of the marzipan on the cake with beaten egg. Press on the balls in a ring round the edge of the cake and brush them with beaten egg.

15. Put the cake on a baking sheet and bake it near to the top of a hot oven, preheated at 230°C for 5 minutes or until nicely tinged brown on top.

Mothering Sunday

In the UK, the Sunday in the middle of Lent is Mothering Sunday. When people had servants to work for them this day was a holiday. It was an opportunity for servants to go home and visit their mothers. They would bake a Simnel cake to take home as a gift as well as picking some of the spring flowers that were just coming into bloom.

Easter eggs

Easter eggs are decorated eggs given at Easter. Of all the symbols associated with Easter, the egg – the symbol of new life – is the most common. Eggs have been used to represent rebirth and new life for hundreds of years, with many customs dating back to ancient traditions.

In the past, people were forbidden from eating eggs during Lent, so it is no surprise that there were lots of eggs to eat when Lent was over.

Egg rolling

The aim of an Easter egg roll is to see who can roll an egg the greatest distance, or who can roll their egg without breaking it. These games usually take place on a grassy slope. It is believed that eggs are rolled downhill as a symbol of the stone being rolled away from the tomb where Jesus was laid.

In the USA, the White House Easter egg roll is an annual event dating back to 1878. Presidents since that date have opened the White House grounds to children for egg rolling and other entertainments on Easter Monday.

Pysanky eggs

In Ukraine it is the custom to exchange beautifully decorated Easter eggs on Easter Sunday. These eggs are called pysanky. The decoration is put on by painting wax onto the egg and dipping it in dye. The wax resists the dye so only the part without wax is coloured. The pattern is built up by painting a different part of the egg each time. The patterns and colours on a pysanky egg all have a meaning. They stand for things like health, happiness or wealth. Girls and boys design their eggs and give them to someone they like – a bit like a Valentine's Day card.

The Easter Bunny

In the USA, the Easter Bunny leaves a basket of chocolate eggs and other treats for children on Easter morning. The tradition of Easter bunnies came from German settlers in the USA. In German folklore there is an Easter hare that delivers coloured eggs to good children. In some countries children go from door to door to ask for eggs.

Rabbits have large litters of babies in the spring and are a symbol of new life. Hares (a bit like rabbits) were associated with Eostre, the ancient goddess of spring. Chicks hatching in the spring are another reminder of new life beginning. Over the years the customs have joined together and somehow the Easter bunny has now become the bringer of eggs.

Decorated eggs

Colourful eggs can be given as Easter gifts, or arranged in a basket as pretty Easter decorations.

For these activities you will need a hard-boiled egg or a blown egg (see the cascarones activity on page 31 to find out how to blow an egg).

Make eggs dyed with natural dyes

Instructions:

Red cabbage dyed eggs

1. Put a handful of cabbage onto a small piece of cloth. Put the egg in the middle and wrap the cloth round the egg.

2. Secure with rubber bands.

3. Put the bundle into a small pan of water and boil slowly for 30 minutes.

4. Leave to cool in the pan overnight. When you take off the wrappings the shells will be dyed pretty shades of . . . blue!

Follow the instructions above but with onion skins to dye the eggs a yellowy orange.

You will need:
* eggs (either hard-boiled or blown)
* finely chopped red cabbage
* pieces of cloth
* rubber bands

Make tie-dye eggs

Instructions:

1. Cover the work surface in thick newspaper.
2. Pour the vinegar onto the kitchen paper. Drip on the food colours.
3. Fold up the egg in the paper. Wrap up with rubber bands.
4. Pour on some water.
5. Put the egg in the egg box to dry overnight.
6. Take off the paper.

You will need:
* eggs (either hard-boiled or blown)
* newspaper and kitchen paper
* 3 teaspoons white vinegar
* 250ml water
* food colouring
* rubber bands

Make crazy striped eggs

Instructions:

1. Twist the rubber bands round the egg.
2. Mix the vinegar, water and food colouring in a bowl.
3. Put the egg in the bowl.
4. Leave for at least 2 hours – the longer you leave it the deeper the colour.
5. Take out of the bowl and leave to dry.
6. Take off the bands to reveal crazy stripes.

You will need:
* eggs (either hard-boiled or blown)
* wide rubber bands
* 3 teaspoons white vinegar
* 250ml water
* food colouring
* a bowl

29

Make an Easter egg tree

An Easter egg tree is a perfect way to display your decorated eggs.

You will need:
- a strong branch with lots of small twigs
- flowerpot to hold the branch
- playdough
- a large needle
- very narrow ribbon
- beads
- decorated blown eggs

Instructions:

1. Push the playdough into the flowerpot.

2. Push the branch into the playdough.

3. Using a large needle, thread a piece of narrow ribbon through the eggs.

4. Tie a bead onto the bottom end of the ribbon, and tie a knot in the ribbon.

5. Tie the ribbons onto the twigs.

JOKE!
Why shouldn't you tell an Easter egg a good joke?

Because it might crack up!

30

Cascarones

A cascarone is an egg shell filled with confetti, then resealed. At Easter time children in Mexico, Spain, Italy and parts of the USA break the eggs above people's heads and shower them with confetti. Lots of fun!

Make cascarones

Instructions:

You will need:
* eggs
* a large safety pin
* a bowl
* confetti
* tissue paper
* glue

1. Undo the safety pin. Use the sharp point to poke a hole in the top (thinner end) of the egg.

2. Make a hole in the opposite end of the egg. This hole should be a bit bigger than the one in the top. Push the pin in as far as you can to break the yolk of the egg and make it easier to blow.

3. Hold the egg over the bowl. Blow through the hole in the top of the egg as if you are blowing up a balloon. The egg will come out of the shell into the bowl.

4. Thoroughly rinse the eggshell and leave to dry.

5. Colour the egg (see pp28–9).

6. When the egg is dry, fill with confetti.

7. Cut a circle of tissue paper. Glue it over the hole in the egg.

Now find someone who doesn't mind having the egg cracked above their head!

Easter cards

Many people send Easter cards to wish each other a 'Happy Easter' and good wishes for the spring season. Here are some ideas for cards that you can make.

Make an Easter chick card

Instructions:

1. Fold a piece of thin card in half to the size you want your finished card to be.

2. Cut out an egg shape from the white card that will fit on the front of the card. Draw round the egg shape onto the yellow paper.

3. Draw an Easter chick inside the egg shape on the yellow paper. Cut out your Easter chick. Decorate the white egg shape in any colours or patterns you like and then cut a zig-zag line across the egg shape, creating two pieces.

You will need:

* yellow paper
* thin card
* white card
* a split pin
* scissors
* felt-tip pens, crayons or paint

4. Glue the chick to the front of the card and then glue the bottom of the egg shape over the bottom of the chick.

5. Ask an adult to push the split pin through the bottom left hand edge of the egg top. Then through the top left hand edge of the egg bottom and the card. Open out the split pin at the back.

The top of the Easter egg will move back to open the egg and reveal the chick.

Make an Easter bunny card

Instructions:

1. Fold the card in half.

2. With the fold at the top, draw the face of a bunny with the ears touching the fold and the chin touching the bottom of the card. Cut round the face up to the fold.

3. Tease out the cotton wool and glue it over the front of the face.

4. Cut out a snout from the pink card and glue onto the bunny face.

5. Cut pink shapes for the inside of the ears. Glue them on the ears.

6. Glue on the beads for the eyes.

7. Cut the straws into three. Flatten them and glue them to the face as whiskers.

Don't forget to write your Easter message inside the card!

EASTER BUNNY FACTS

Originally Easter was associated with the hare not the rabbit. Over time the rabbit (or bunny) took over as they are more commonly seen.

Rabbits are a symbol of new life as they have lots of babies. A pair of rabbits can have up to 20 babies (kits) at a time and up to eight litters a year. That is a lot of bunnies!

JOKE!

How does the Easter Bunny stay fit?

Eggs-ercise and hare-robics!

Sweets and treats

As well as chocolate eggs, many other delicious treats are made at Easter. Chocolate nests are both decorative and very tasty! Easter biscuits use up ingredients that may not be eaten during Lent. They are bigger than normal biscuits, making them a big treat!

Make Easter egg nests

Ingredients:
- 75g cornflakes
- 100g chocolate
- mini eggs
- 50g butter
- 2 tbsp golden syrup

You will need:
- a microwave-proof bowl
- a wooden spoon
- cake cases
- fluffy chicks

Instructions:

1. Break the chocolate into pieces and put them in a bowl with the butter and golden syrup.

2. Ask an adult to melt the chocolate in the microwave for 30 seconds. Alternatively get help in melting the chocolate in a bowl sitting above a pan of boiling water.

3. Mix the cornflakes into the chocolate, being careful not to crush them too much.

4. When the cornflakes are all coated with chocolate, spoon some of the mixture into each cake case.

5. Make a hollow in the middle with the back of a spoon.

6. Put mini eggs into the hollow.

7. Put in the fridge to set.

8. Decorate with little fluffy Easter chicks.

Make Easter biscuits

You will need:
* a large bowl
* a fork
* a tablespoon
* a rolling pin
* large cookie cutter
* two baking trays
* wire cooling rack

Ingredients:
* 100g soft butter
* 75g caster sugar
* 1 egg yolk
* 200g plain flour
* half a teaspoon mixed spice
* half a teaspoon ground cinnamon
* 75g currants
* 2 tbsp caster sugar
* 1 tbsp milk

Instructions:

1. Turn the oven dial to 200°C.

2. Using a wooden spoon mix together the butter and sugar in a large bowl.

3. Beat in the egg yolk.

4. Add the flour, spices and currants and mix them in.

5. Add a tablespoon of milk. It should be a soft dough that will roll out but not be too sticky.

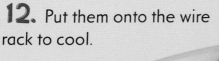

6. Spread a bit of flour on the work surface. Roll out the dough until it's about 5mm thick.

7. Using a large cookie cutter, cut out shapes.

8. Squish any leftover bits together and roll them out again until all the dough is cut out.

9. Put the biscuits onto two baking trays.

10. Ask a grown-up to put the trays into the oven for 10-15 minutes until they are lightly golden and then take them out.

11. Sprinkle them with caster sugar while they are still warm.

12. Put them onto the wire rack to cool.

Easter gifts

In the USA, the Easter Bunny gives children a basket of Easter eggs and other gifts. A pretty gift basket can be filled with decorated eggs, Easter biscuits tied with a pretty bow, or other small gifts.

Make a gift basket

Instructions:

1. Draw two lines on the card joining up the opposite corners.

2. Measure 12cm along the diagonal lines from each corner.

3. Cut along the line.

4. Bend the corners back from the diagonal lines (x8).

5. Fold up the corners with one diagonal flap to the back and one to the front.

6. Glue the flaps together.

7. Cut a strip of card to make a handle.

8. Ask a grown-up to staple the handle on either side of the basket. You can hide the staples with a sticker or some glitter glue.

9. Line the basket with shredded tissue paper.

You will need:
✽ **square piece of card 31cm x 31cm** – printed card looks nice or you can decorate your own with stickers and glitter.
✽ **glue**
✽ **a stapler**
✽ **shredded tissue paper**

Fill with goodies for your friends or family.

Fabergé eggs

Peter Carl Fabergé was jeweller and goldsmith to the Russian Imperial Court. Between 1885 and 1917 he made many fabulous jewelled golden eggs. All the eggs were richly decorated with enamel and precious gems. Each egg was unique, and each one opened to reveal a secret. Some had moving parts, others contained tiny paintings or sculptures, clocks or replicas of ships and coaches.

In 1917, the Russian Revolution forced the House of Fabergé to close, and Peter and his family to flee from Russia. The eggs they made are worth a lot of money and are collectors' items.

You will need:
* ❁ blown egg (see p31)
* ❁ beads ❁ sequins
* ❁ stick on jewels
* ❁ glue ❁ paint

Make a beautiful Fabergé-style decorated egg

Instructions:

1. Paint the egg and leave it to dry.

2. Glue a thin piece of ribbon round the middle of the egg. Glue a thin piece of ribbon at right angles to it.

3. Glue beads, stick on jewels and sequins onto the egg.

4. Finish the egg with a pretty jewel on the top.

Fun with flowers

Spring flowers are very colourful. Bright yellow daffodils, red tulips, pink and blue hyacinths are all out in the spring.

Make these spring flower crafts to give to someone this Easter. They will last much longer than the real thing!

You will need:
- ❀ green paper
- ❀ a wrapped lolly
- ❀ yellow tissue paper
- ❀ a jam jar lid
- ❀ a pencil
- ❀ scissors

Make a sweet daffodil

Instructions:

1. Starting at the corner, roll the green paper up into a tight roll and tape the ends.

2. Draw round the jam jar lid onto the thin card and cut out the shape.

3. Shape the edge of the circle into petals. Cut out and use this shape as a template. Draw round the template onto the tissue paper. Cut out three or four flower shapes and put them together.

4. Make a hole in the centre and push the lolly through the hole.

5. Turn the flower over and push the lolly stick into the roll of paper.

6. Tape the paper tube to the flower petals.

Spring flowers

During spring, many bright and colourful flowers come into bloom - tulips and the yellow daffodil being favourites. In Germany daffodils are called *Osterglocken*, meaning 'Easter bells'. There is a legend that says the daffodil first appeared in the Garden of Gethsemane, on the night Jesus held the Last Supper.

Tulips, originally from Asia, were introduced into Holland in the seventeenth century. They were so expensive that for a time they were treated like a form of currency – a period known as 'tulip mania'. Many countries around the world hold tulip festivals to herald the beginning of spring.

Make a garden of daffodils and tulips

Instructions:

You will need:
- ❀ an egg box
- ❀ coloured paints
- ❀ lolly sticks
- ❀ a bottle cap
- ❀ playdough
- ❀ glue
- ❀ coloured paper
- ❀ a pencil
- ❀ scissors

Paint the egg box green – leave to dry.

Daffodils

1. Draw a daffodil flower on a piece of yellow paper and cut it out. Draw round the shape on a second piece of paper and cut it out.

2. Glue the two pieces of paper together with the lolly stick sandwiched between them.

3. Paint the bottle cap yellow and leave to dry. Glue the bottle top in the centre of the flower. Glue long green petals cut from green paper to the lolly stick.

Tulips

1. Draw a tulip flower on a piece of coloured paper and cut it out. Draw round the shape on a second piece of paper and cut it out. Paint the tulips in a funky pattern and leave to dry.

2. Glue the two pieces of paper together with the lolly stick sandwiched between them.

3. Glue long green leaves cut from green paper to the lolly stick.

4. Push some playdough into the bottom of the egg box.

5. Stick the lolly sticks into the playdough to make a colourful spring flower presentation.

Easter gardens

At Easter some people make Easter gardens. They are made to represent the Garden of Gethsemane, where Jesus spent the night before his crucifixion, the mound upon which he was crucified and the tomb where his body was laid to rest.

An Easter garden has three elements: a mound with a cross, a tomb and flowers and greenery. Easter gardens can be made for homes or can be a focal point in a church.

Make an Easter garden

You will need:
- a shallow tray or dish
- garden soil, moss, twigs
- a flat stone
- empty yoghurt pot
- egg cups ✿ flowers
- small stones ✿ string

Instructions:

1. Fill the tray with soil.

2. Push the soil up on one side of the tray to make a hill.

3. Press the empty yoghurt pot into the side of the hill to make a tomb.

4. Cover the soil with moss.

5. Tie twigs together to make three crosses. Set them into the top of the hill.

6. Place the stone over the mouth of the tomb.

7. Make a path coming from the tomb with small stones.

8. Decorate the garden with egg cups filled with flowers.

Easter egg hunt

In some countries, the Easter Bunny hides eggs for children to find. These are called Easter egg hunts. They are great fun and you may want to plan your own. Here are some suggestions of what you could do:

❋ Ask someone who is not going to be hunting to hide lots of little wrapped chocolate eggs in the house and garden and see who can find the most in a given amount of time. You could cut out egg shapes from coloured paper and hide those instead of chocolate eggs.

❋ Give a prize to the person that finds the most.

❋ To make your Easter egg hunt more interesting, try making up clues and writing them on slips of paper and then get people to work them out.

❋ Play 'hotter and colder'. Hide a chocolate egg so that everyone but the person hunting knows where it is. When they begin the hunt say 'colder' more and more quietly as they get further away or 'hotter' louder and louder as they get closer to an egg. Each person gets a turn to be the hunter, so make sure you have plenty of eggs!

JOKE!
Why did the Easter egg hide?

Because he was a little chicken!

Easter parades

Easter Day parades are held in cities all over the USA, but the Fifth Avenue parade in New York is the most famous. People wear their best clothes and extravagant Easter bonnets.

The tradition of Easter bonnets comes from wearing colourful flowers in a hat to celebrate Easter Sunday after wearing very plain, dull clothes during Lent.

Look at the colourful Easter bonnets below and have a go at making your own.

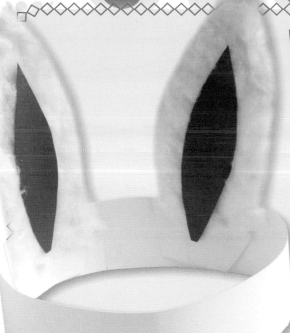

Make a rabbit ears hat

You will need:
* thin white card
* pink paper
* scissors
* a pencil
* sticky tape
* cotton wool
* glue

Instructions:

1. Cut a strip of white card about 5cm wide and long enough to wrap round your head and overlap by 2cm.

2. Using sticky tape join the band together to fit comfortably round your head.

3. Cut two ears out of white card each about 20cm long x 8cm wide. Cover them in glue and cotton wool.

4. Cut two smaller ears out of pink paper.

5. Glue the pink ears inside the white ears.

6. Glue the ears inside the band either side of the join.

You will need:
* raffia or brown/gold tissue paper cut into thin strips
* a paper plate
* ribbon
* feathers
* chocolate eggs
* glue
* brown paint
* scissors

Make a bird's nest hat

Instructions:

1. Paint the plate brown. Leave to dry.

2. Ask a grown-up to make a slit in opposite sides of the paper plate and thread the ribbon through. Leave the ends long enough to tie under your chin.

3. Take a handful of raffia or strips of tissue paper and bend it into a circle to fit on the plate. Spread some glue round the edge of the plate. Place the nest of raffia on the glue. Put a magazine on top to hold it down. Leave it to dry.

4. When it is dry, glue on some feathers.

5. Glue the chocolate eggs onto the middle of the plate and leave everything to dry.

To wear your bonnet, tie the ribbons under your chin.

Easter quiz

How much do you really know about Easter? Be an Easter eggspert and teach your friends lots of interesting Easter facts. All the answers are somewhere in this book

✸ What are the days leading up to Easter called?

✸ How did Jesus arrive in Jerusalem?

✸ Where did Jesus spend the night before he died?

✸ Who found Jesus' empty tomb?

✸ What is the day before Lent called?

✸ What are traditionally eaten on the day before Lent?

✸ Who made jewelled eggs for the Russian Imperial Court?

✸ Who delivers baskets of treats to children in the USA?

✸ What do the people in Ukraine call the decorated eggs that they exchange at Easter?

Easter egg hunt!

There are 10 of these blue spotted Easter eggs hidden in this book.

HOW MANY CAN YOU FIND?

Index